ENDURING WEALTH

ENDURING WEALTH

LEONARD CRIMSON

CONTENTS

1 Introduction to Long-Term Investing   1

2 The Foundation: Setting Financial Goals   5

3 Building Blocks of Long-Term Investing   9

4 Risk Management Strategies   13

5 Evaluating Investment Opportunities   17

6 Developing a Long-Term Investment Strategy   21

7 Psychology of Investing   23

8 Monitoring and Adjusting Your Investments   27

9 Impact of Economic Trends on Long-Term Investments
31

10 Ethical and Sustainable Investing   33

11 Investing in Emerging Markets   35

12 Real Estate as a Long-Term Investment   39

13 Retirement Planning and Long-Term Investing   41

14 Legacy Planning and Generational Wealth   45

15 Case Studies in Successful Long-Term Investing   49

16 Conclusion: The Journey Ahead   53

CHAPTER 1

Introduction to Long-Term Investing

Investing is all about deferring today's consumption and putting off the immediate gratification of spending money in the hope of having more (and sometimes much more) stuff than you could have had otherwise. One of the main appeals of long-term investing is that it can help provide enduring wealth. Enduring wealth—where investment returns are bedrocks of intergenerational capital foundations—is not built overnight. Your first steps as an investor would be best taken in a time frame equivalent to the investment horizon you will need to successfully design, build, run, and eventually adapt a family dynasty.

Depending on the level of wealth, a grand strategy might involve the deployment of investment pools to eke out enough inflation-plus-return potential to help mitigate the complexities of inflating operating costs. Inflows from joint-profit projects could then pay for extraordinary life events, including those hailed as sending the kids to 'good' schools (whatever good might really mean), aged care, and medical access. And then there is an aspirational edge to long-term investing. It can be used to build a philanthropic capital pool to help heal societies, empower the powerless, and protect the planet. Making a philanthropic investment alone, however, does not entitle an investor to handpick the social currency the recipient should spend; that is not truly philanthropic. The practical impetus behind every major portfolio build is operational effectiveness. In the case of a philanthropic infrastructure, do your heirs even have families? If they do, are they well? If they are well, are they wise about the world and the people that reside within it? The philosophical thrust behind philanthropic investing cannot be simply a last will and testament that funds specific types of social inputs.

Definition and Principles
Defined by Benjamin Graham as an operation that "assumes as its basic concept that the future value of the investment is determined with a high degree of accuracy (irrespective of personal throughout everyone's lifetimes, both career-wise, and in investing).

The Cornerstones of Wealth Creation

The preparation to be a long-term investor starts with the accumulation of savings. This means to carefully withhold a part of your income which you will invest. The first success criteria in investing is that you have to have the means to do it. This is how the vast majority of people actually get into the market. It's not by having a great idea to invest in a specific stock. So "Save early and often" must be one of the central pillars of wealth creation, including investing. Second, one of the most essential principles in long-term investing is a reasonably well-developed investment philosophy. This is fundamental and has to be established before you get into any kind of investment. Forming an investment philosophy is all about creating a set of beliefs and understandings that help you to keep calm and relatively rational amidst all of the stresses of investing. To reach such a level of self-awareness, you require a thorough understanding of the gone, which would include the history of financial markets in general, and your investment in a particular sector. You will never get under the skin of the market if you truly don't have an interest in financial history.

Before undertaking any form of financial transactions, an individual has to have an understanding of him or herself and answer the questions related to individual temperament and risk tolerance. Are you someone who can calmly hold a stock for years as it emits Crag values five times larger than the stock price? Or are you someone who gets irritated when an investment hasn't worked out over six months and is inclined to sell based on market sentiment rather than rational logic? Unless these psychological aspects are understood by the individual, it is risky and idle to invest.

CHAPTER 2

The Foundation: Setting Financial Goals

The bedrock foundation for the kind of long-term investing strategy we'll discuss in this book is money management from the standpoint of setting and achieving financial goals. If you don't have any financial goals that you can articulate and that you believe you'll achieve someday, it is difficult to find a lot of meaning in stock picking and asset allocation. If, on the other hand, you have a system for dealing with your personal finances that develops very specific goals and a plan to reach them, the successful execution of your investment strategy gets a lot simpler. Running a family's personal finances in this way helps individuals, couples, and families attain their goals and experience overwhelming financial success. I know this because my family has been using it as part of our long-term investing strategy for more than four decades. You may ask what long-term financial success and the successful execution of an investment strategy have to do with each other. Much more than you might think.

When individuals, couples, and families are successful in running their end-of-the-month financial systems, individually tailored financial goals can be integrated into a stock portfolio. Family entrepreneurs who are running their end-of-the-month financial system with great success are ready to begin long-term investing because they have learned to live within their means in such a way that they put 10% of their discretionary income toward financial independence.

Understanding Personal Finance

When it comes to long-term investing or building wealth over time, personal finance reigns king. Personal finance is the key to each and every strategy there is out there to build wealth long-term. Personal finance can be complicated. Dave Ramsey, Suze Orman, etc. want to make things simple, but it's just not a simple subject. However, it is crucial that we take the time to understand our finances as in doing so we are setting the groundwork to be in a position to build wealth by the act of long-term investing.

In this post, I'm going to explain my personal journey in long-term investing. My journey began with choosing a degree which would bring me a nice income at an affordable cost, to obtaining student loans, keeping expenses low and investing anything extra. Your finance and investing journey probably don't look like mine, but there are possibly moments we may share. I grew up in a middle-class family of 6. I learned at a very young age the importance of hard work and "making money." When I was about 12 years old, I found envelopes of $100 cash stashed around my room. My dad came in one evening, sat down on my bed, and we had a long talk about personal finance. That $100 cash was from the previous summer; by handing my dad my summer job paychecks, he put that cash away for me in an IRA. Mom and Dad gave me my first "lesson" in long-term investing long before I knew what that was. Budget! University tuition was paid for by my parents, but my expenses were up to me. I worked four different jobs all through college so that, combined with student loans, I would be comfortable. My BA in finance was very valuable; I could have flown to New Zealand for 2 years and still pay off my loans easily. I found an extraordinary company and decided to stay. I took the remaining money, about $100,000 at the time, and paid off my debt, maxing a Roth IRA and 401(k) my personal goal. It took me one year to become completely debt-free.

CHAPTER 3

Building Blocks of Long-Term Investing

I first discussed the value of patience as one of five core philosophies that should steer our actions. The power of patience was on full display this week during the IPOs of Paytm and Rivian. Next, I identified nine items that I always keep in mind when making a new investment. The first three steps to long-term investing are laid within these nine: find a company with an unfair advantage, identify its growth opportunity, and understand its financials well enough to project cash flow. Finally, I have outlined five important steps for getting new purchases right, which is the emotional aspect to investing that cannot be overstated.

When I was in school, I thought that the secret to investing was technical analysis. After studying the subject for years, however, I decided that the future is just not something that we can predict. This realization does not mean that there aren't building blocks to long-term investing. There are. They include having a philosophy, choosing the right amount of money to invest at the beginning, finding something truly great to invest in, constantly asking ourselves whether we should hold the assets that we have or reinvest in something else, and having the critical ability to stick to our plan. We will delve deeper into these points below, but the cornerstone is patience – the subject of my latest Business Bullpen edition.

The first key to investing, before we make any decisions at all, is to truly have a philosophy behind what we want to do with our money. If we start from emotion and simply buy because things are going up, we will eventually get scared and run for the exit after they go down. It is with philosophy in mind that we can then apply some rational thought and preserve wealth.

Asset Classes and Diversification

The first principle of fundamental long-term investing is the ownership of financial assets. Common asset classes of financial assets are stocks, bonds, investment real estate (sometimes referred to as direct participation in a real estate partnership or hard assets), and cash and equivalents. Foundational to reducing the risk of owning stocks and increasing returns is the concept of diversification. Historically, there has been a high correlation between owning a variety of asset classes, even on an international scale. However, owning a variety of asset classes within the country of domicile can enhance wealth while reducing relative risk.

Diversification can slip away in as little as 24 hours, as witnessed over the last few years (October 2007 to March 9, 2009), if care is not paid to consistently rebalance. Yet in the previous 75 years leading to the beginning of the recent market slide, diversified portfolios have increased wealth. This brings us to one key of fundamental investing, which is to ignore temporary roller-coaster rides and adhere to the patient long-term investing process. Even in the short term, however, diversification pays. As one asset class is decreasing in value, another might be holding its ground or appreciating. Petrol reaches $40 a barrel one day, only to decline to $18 a barrel two weeks later (in 2001). Diversification is never as "sexy" as the hard story of the millions made by investing in the initial stock offering of Microsoft or Google. But the last laugh, however, is on the side of the disciplined investor; for over time, long-term diversification has been shown to build wealth. We have strong historic reasons for professing our approach to investing.

CHAPTER 4

Risk Management Strategies

R isk management is a major priority.

In the long run, short-term investment is essentially an arbitrage proposition. Higher returns require higher risks or higher inconvenience. They are no less work - just as different as earning a living through a 9-to-5 job and starting one's own business that requires 24/7 involvement. So it's one and the same business in different forms. Do what works best for you. For most of us - and Warren Buffett has always pointed out some important business interests at a time - it's a simple investment. LBO, hedge funds, commodity funds, day trading, value investing, investing in high-growth stocks or start-up companies, investing in classic growth stocks or growth at a decent price (GARP) stocks can all coexist. Sure there are overlaps - but these strategy divisions illustrate there are many roads to the promised land. What's missing in this whole definition is the management of risks - something extremely important when it comes to protecting portfolio value. So let's discuss this in-depth - it's the real juice of successful long-term investing.

Risk is a fundamental consideration for all investors, and there are multiple strategies for managing it. The bottom line, however, doesn't need to be complicated. These strategies intend to manage the human heart's insatiable hunt for greater value (greed) and abhorrence of high (both sweeping and targeted) losses. Sometimes it helps to stand back from finance and invest entirely for a while, I think. In the end, the best values arise during the panic period when short-sighted purchases flee the field, out of favor. Stuff then bounces back, and reasonable returns are understood, although not necessary. Wouldn't it hurt to have a lower profit on a regular basis? Utility and flexibility must also be relative to action. If there is something in the portfolio that you don't need immediately, you can also own it and prefer a higher risk or volatility.

Importance of Risk Assessment

Risk Assessment For many, the only way to lose money in the stock market is to get out before they have been invested for a sufficiently long period, says the American financier Seth Klarman about the value of holding equity investments for the long term. His observation raises several important questions: what exactly is sufficient when applied to time? What are the risks one takes in any investment that hinges on the playing out of time? And what is the reward for accepting those risks? These are not complicated questions and they are the ones that I am going to discuss in the following pages of this paper.

Clearly, when control is a prime consideration, wealth preservation becomes synonymous with ensuring that the associated investment returns are of a real and enduring nature. For those who are attempting to acquire, compound, and distribute the wealth (property) of other people, it would make no sense to do so with an investment plan that cannot endure. A major step toward putting one's capital in a position to endure is to study very closely the investments that one makes, with more attention being paid to the risks that an investment carries than to its money-making potential, and to seek to build as much of a safety net as possible by adding King's Ransoms to the asset base to increase the chances that the wealth being relied on is not eroded in real terms.

CHAPTER 5

Evaluating Investment Opportunities

I have tried to isolate a few key principles as guides to choosing investments. However, the choices are nearly infinite, and every investment is unique, so my discussion of those principles is not as useful as it could be. (The expanded explanation of those criteria might be interesting as a launchpad for further thinking, though.) But what could always be valuable are guidelines for the process of selecting investments and, indeed, for determining how to identify a good investment. (I suggest only rudimentary current thinking on this.) Since the most common activities center on securities, I will here try to tackle the initial stages of evaluating one of those investment opportunities. However, many of the ideas apply more broadly perhaps to picking private company investments.

The fundamentalist employs either categories of businesses through valuation or categorizes firms more by those with brighter versus duller prospects. Only those firms are to be bought that are fundamentally undervalued or have an appreciated purchase value that is markedly less than its potential value to a future purchaser. The technician, on the other hand, believes that all information about the company available to those on the inside of the company is known by the market and reflected in the current market price quoted on the wall boards. To the technical analyst, both IBM and Ramajay Electronics Incorporated are nothing but lines and dots on graph paper from which to divine future price movements. For him there is no distinction to be found between investments.

Fundamental vs. Technical Analysis

There are generally two camps of investment analysis. The first camp is fundamental analysis, which includes examining a company's income statement, balance sheet, cash flow statement, and management. In addition, an analyst will also look at the trends occurring within a sector, often employing a Porter's Five Forces framework to understand the nature of an industry and whether or not it is attractive to invest in. The second camp is technical analysis, which is analysis based primarily on price action. Adherents to this form of analysis believe that "the market consists of trends which can be possibly identified and employed" to turn a quick profit. They also believe that "the market discounts everything," arguing that a trader can look at the information in a chart solely because the price action will tell the person everything about the stock, option, future, or currency. There are some weaknesses to this form of thinking when considering the stock market, though. Primarily, most stock markets enjoy positive trends rather than bear markets (markets that demonstrate continuous declines), although these do exist and tend to last much longer than many of the shorter-term mutual funds some of the traders invest in.

Why are these forms of analysis relevant to us discussing enduring capital? We believe in the fundamental analysis of stocks and markets as a whole. We also believe that technical analysis is (sometimes) a self-fulfilling prophecy, although in relation to longer-term investments, we think they mean little to nothing. Fundamental analysis is attractive to us in the sense that as the economy keeps growing, eventually the market will hit a bottom (or undergo a bear market correction), which will create value opportunities when things look like they are in fact on their way up - like they currently are.

CHAPTER 6

Developing a Long-Term Investment Strategy

In constructing your initial portfolio, you need to think about a proper balance between speculative and high-quality investments and discuss it with your advisor. Like most of the elements in your overall strategy, an investment portfolio should be designed to reflect your individual needs, goals, and attitude toward risk.

One of the most important things to remember in investing is that the moment when you first buy a security should be the moment when you've made up your mind to keep it for life. When you buy a common stock, recognize that you are buying or acquiring at least a little piece of a business. Purchase on the same principles as you would use in buying a good business: (1) the right price, (2) the highest possible value. Determine if the stock is a "buy" by estimating its "intrinsic" value (underlying value) rather than watching the "momentum" of the stock price. Apply the same common sense to your purchase of securities as you would to any other major purchase in your life. If you buy your shares with this business perspective, you will retain your interest in the company. You will attend company meetings, read the annual reports, and serve as a monitor for the corporate executives.

Creating a Balanced Portfolio

Finally, choosing a balanced portfolio is certainly a key part of everyone's investment strategy. It may not be the perfect choice of assets for everyone, but the general concept is that it satisfies every investor's investment goal of earning high returns easily and sustainably. I believe even small investors should consider creating a balanced portfolio. In other words, everyone should participate in investing by putting at least some of their money, maybe 20 percent of their wealth, in equity. The conventional thinking is that liquidity preferences are too strong, so most investors choose to put their money in a fixed maturity of a certificate of deposit (CD) in preference to buying stocks.

They fear that investing in stocks may prove to be unlucky if they are forced to sell soon – and that might easily happen simply by getting a pink slip, having an illness, or just needing the money for tuition, a car repair, or whatever. And that can happen at almost any time, starting with big losses within a few months after making the new investment. Or so the thinking goes! However, if you can construct a "balanced portfolio" for everyone that makes sense. Everyone – young and old – investing for the long run should allocate a fixed number of dollars to each investment sector – large or small common stocks and short or long-term bonds. This smoothes the effect risk of a stock-mobbed portfolio. So there is a sense to "normalizing" the investment that gives small investors no more and no less than the market average.

CHAPTER 7

Psychology of Investing

Psychological aspects of investing

Psychological studies of investing have shown that people employ a variety of simulation and estimation methods when making their decisions. These studies fall into two domains of inquiry to explain financial anomalies: traditional inquiry, primarily led by economic theory, and behavioral inquiry.

The traditional finance of economic and financial experts tends to concentrate on the "rational investor" and the appraisal of risk and returns based on market fundamentals. Behavioral finance, however, focuses on the relevance of irrational psychological factors that impact decision-making in the financial markets. Behavioral finance contradicts the theory of traditional finance that long-run equilibrium in asset and stock markets does exist. By illustrating how some investors' subjective perception deviates from the prices established by the stock market, behavioral finance describes various financial anomalies that currently exist.

According to psychologists, investors have cognitive biases, personality traits, and emotional motivations that play a role in determining investment attitudes and risk appetite. Behavioral finance points out that the primary mental hurdles of rational decision-making occur because fixed and long-established rules of thumb based on their development of emotions and mental wiring exist. Consequently, people's decisions can be much more dogmatic and bound by their history and unconsciously or consciously held biases and beliefs than experts believe.

The most common biases include confirmation bias, or the tendency towards looking for evidence to confirm one's existing convictions, and anchoring, a psychological tendency to deter decision-makers from recalibrating their understanding. Indeed, psychology shows that investors can put things in a context that makes them more economical to engage in. Thus, it is clear that psychological factors significantly influence stock price formation so that the stock market is not always efficient.

Behavioral Biases and Decision-Making

A lazy golf caddie offers a player two clubs instead of one because he cannot remember the proper distance for a seven-iron. The author of this story, George Will, writes that neural efficiency is the key to understanding this episode. Neural efficiency is the ability to solve complex problems faster than is warranted. People can make inferences in statistically reliable ways better than a multiple regression equation using limited cognitive resources. Such successes are not always perfect, however. The golfer can make the one inference out of 999,999 correct, George Will explains. These flawed inferences arise because of the mental shortcuts that each person makes.

These shortcuts help people manage the complex amount of information they deal with each day. Consequently, the normal work of the mind is pervaded with "effortless perceptions, judgments, and decisions that conceal, thinly cloaked, their cognitive and emotional origins," Daniel Kahneman writes in his book, Thinking, Fast and Slow. The hidden influence of emotion on decisions is of particular relevance when making changes to a long-term investment approach. Money is a source of insecurity, easily linked with concerns about a person's self-worth. Meanwhile, most people have a herd instinct that draws them to conventional, widely held beliefs about culture and society. Cognitive and emotional biases can combine into a heightened sensitivity to feedback from the market; the more people monitor the news and talk to their global network of investors, bankers, asset managers, and other contacts, the more dissonance they develop in their minds. These individual biases have the potential to undermine long-term performance.

CHAPTER 8

Monitoring and Adjusting Your Investments

As part of my new step-by-step process of long-term investing, one of the most important areas of focus has been around the process of monitoring and potentially adjusting our investments after the initial portfolio was selected. In this installment of this series on long-term investing, let's dive into those steps.

For me, the next step that should be a part of any framework for long-term investing is rebalancing or adjusting your portfolio. Second, keep an eye on taxes and always remember why you are buying or selling an investment.

Rebalancing your portfolio is code for selling your winners, taking that money, and using it to buy more of your losers. When the dust settled after I chose an asset allocation and fund in Article 3 and looked where I stood with my chosen investments, large cap stocks were a clear outperformer. That pushed us over the 80% stocks I originally wanted our portfolio to have and we needed to move it back down to a maximum of 80%. This is the first of two small adjustments I plan to make each time I look at our portfolio. For the bigger overall adjustments, I will allow my allocation to drift a little more before making a trade. On top of rebalancing, I decided to look at the performance of our entire portfolio at the same time.

Rebalancing and Tax Considerations

Rebalancing

The two most important considerations when managing money are to maintain an objective basis and to restrain temptation (discussed in depth in the conclusion of this letter). Portfolio rebalancing is the cornerstone of putting this principle into practice. The primary goal of enduring wealth is preserved capital. Consequently, I personally abhor a sizable allocation to equities because I see little room for maintaining the objective of preserved capital under such a circumstance. But that is hardly relevant to the majority of clients at our firm with 50, 60, 70, and even 100% allocations to equities. We never perceive a bubble. Everyone else does. We do have our principles. One of those is that we avoid the noise and concentrate on only a few specific things heavily. We will not sacrifice our objectivity for a 70% asset allocation. We will, for purely subjective reasons, only make mild recommendations regarding prime funds (de facto equities) for a 4-5% slice of the portfolio. Remember that, firstly, the goal is preserved capital and secondly, in the alternative world that we live in, we have to pursue it by taking measured steps that challenge credulity. The back-up plans are measured and put only in place in the necessary areas.

Tax Considerations

And that brings us to the second important consideration of a principled money manager. When possible, it is always necessary to take into account the altered tax implications in every portfolio management decision. For example, stocks recently shed the gains built up after January and fell into negative territory Year-to-Date. If we sold, taking a 2% loss for the year, we would actually have a 3-3.5%

cash portfolio and a 2% loss in our stock portfolio that could then be balanced out with our 5.5% prime. So, each $100 dollars I invested is now worth $95. However, if I take the time to transfer my funds to cash automatically, I am left with gains in my stock that I incurred the cost of selling shares of stock. I would be left with more money under this scenario.

CHAPTER 9

Impact of Economic Trends on Long-Term Investments

Economic trends have very different impacts on long-term investment strategies compared to short-term market movements. Beyond this, the rise of globalization and the proliferation of international investments have also substantially changed the composition of the stock market worldwide. Investors now have a choice of home-country and international financial markets, real estate, cryptocurrency, precious metals, and many other potential investments. This increases the inherent competition between these investment choices and places limits on what any single market can truly offer. This can be partially mitigated through diversification, which is made more feasible by the great amount of information and ease of transactions that we now have, but there is real uncertainty about whether this will be enough to maintain the long-run performance of the United States. Moreover, as more countries open their borders to international investment, one could expect the performance of their stock markets to gradually mean-revert: as investors become more able to buy foreign stocks, their prices should rise, reducing their expected returns. This could also reflect national differences in law and culture. But only time will tell whether the world's markets will behave more or less rationally in the future than the United States or any other individual financial market has in the past.

Global Market Dynamics

It is because of the dynamics of global markets that opportunities often arise, and the fact that different macro conditions create assets at different valuations. But opportunities in equities constantly oscillate due to market volatility, trends, shocks, and patterns. This generality is true because time varies constantly. So, the point isn't that we just need time or that we need a fixed period. Effects can differ with different periods if we consider the fluctuations and cycles in different parts of the period. As a long-term investor, it is also difficult to handle economic and policy change, since financial market dynamics ignore it by being optimistic and pessimistic.

An investor's performance depends a lot on when and how they invest. All businesses go through cycles and also face shocks. Each crisis was unique, but there are also recurring factors in all crises. So, interest rates paid in a low-inflationary economy are so different from rates in high-growth, high-inflationary periods. Policies also differ in various directions due to conventional or unconventional changes in the global financial industry or non-financial changes in consumer demand and fiscal and monetary branches. As I indicated above, we need simple, understandable but stable assets to have a long-term investment strategy that can grow and maintain its wealth over time. A good trustee can reinvest the returns and raise the purchasing power of his mandate or cope with inflation. What could have more stability than participation in well-run companies that produce goods that are consumable across the globe?

CHAPTER 10

Ethical and Sustainable Investing

For companies to flourish in the long run, they must have good ethical values at their core. It is only by investing in companies that put people and the planet before profit that we will see a truly sustainable future. Overcompany management frequently changes, but a mission statement is static and should be our guiding principle. In the long term, the best-performing companies will fully embrace this principle. Of course, we can "invest" in ethical funds, and there are a few that have been performing well over the last 20 years. However, these are managed using computer algorithms, "momentum models," that focus on the share price performance of a company rather than their actual values or ethics. If the share price of an ethical company falls, then the fund will sell because the computer thinks that it is no longer ethical.

We invest in companies that are genuinely creating a sustainable and positive future for us all. The fact that we are very bullish long term does not mean that we believe all companies are good value. "Dark factories" is a term used to describe high-value companies that are performing well in that focuses on big data, intellectual property, and other 'non-tangibles'. In the long run, many companies that manufacture anything can't compete with those that operate dark factories. A classic example is the differences between Excel and GM. The former operates more like a marketing company, focused on brands, low fixed capital value, and higher net profits. This is why the company has a higher price-to-earnings ratio. GM, on the other hand, operates a capital asset-heavy business, focused on automobiles and car dealerships. The difference between the two companies is the intrinsic value of the companies via Directors' Pay & Performance.

Environmental, Social, and Governance (ESG) Factors

Sustainability. Many portfolio managers are incorporating ESG factors as part of their stock selection or investment decision-making process when choosing which companies to invest in.

The relevance of ESG factors to long-term investors is that other investors also pay attention and, as a result, will affect the price of the company. If you are a long-term value investor, you should analyze ESG factors in your stock selection process. As more people start investing with ESG and other long-term factors in mind, the future cash flows will be affected. For example, people do not behave the same way when they consume in terms of impact. This will affect companies' sales, expenses, employees' health and environment, among others, which will affect the profits of companies, and all such shortfalls will drive stock prices down. Hence, if you are buying the shares of these companies, you need to take this into account as you will be affected too. Therefore, ESG factors are important in value creation. Companies that create long-term value for shareholders have good attention to ESG issues. Therefore, ESG factors should be examined in stock selection to add another comparative aspect to the fundamental analysis of potential investments.

CHAPTER 11

Investing in Emerging Markets

A significant proportion of my investing career in the 1980s was spent in emerging markets. I should emphasize at the outset that investing in developing countries is highly specialized and has unique characteristics not encountered investing in the US, Europe, or other advanced countries. Indeed, many of the special skills and advantages which the analytical investor and his advisers can fully utilize in other markets, especially the US, are of limited value or availability and in most cases are simply irrelevant in the emerging area. Our overall policy for investing in emerging markets, like that for more advanced countries, was a long-term one. This strategy is eminently sensible in nations whose future growth prospects are the most exciting. So long as the country improved its economic and political structure - or at least moved not too far in the opposite direction, as Iran did with the outcome we have already discussed - we felt under almost any circumstances that eventually our investment would be successful. An example would be the belief in West Germany increasing in the 1940s.

Our sales policy was not systematic, but relied heavily on our anticipation of an impending bear market or the possible outbreak of hostilities. We have already mentioned our success in selling when our local confidence index went too high. I can now think of major sales that we should have made in our early, prideful days when we were overconfident about the future returns of an investment. One thing is clear, any investor who lacks patience will continue to make the same senseless moves in the developing countries that are made by the ordinary investors in the US and elsewhere. Many of the commonplaces of Wall Street would change their form completely if they were issued with future topical investments and short selling prohibited.

Opportunities and Challenges

Here I intentionally use the word "investing," as opposed to trading, specifically referencing the long-term investment focus, the powerful theme of this book. Over the past half-century, foreign markets in Asia have presented American investors with enormous opportunities, from Japan through the "Four Tigers" and now to the "Four Markets." With huge GDP growth rates in countries such as India, resource-based markets like Indonesia (the largest Muslim nation), and the global low-cost production center of Vietnam, the emerging markets will continue to be powerful investment themes for the rest of this century. I share a number of specific opportunities that I'd present to you or your gift recipients if I were as dashing and debonair as a financial newsletter writer. Finally, since no investment is all upside, I discuss some of the significant risks or challenges that investors need to be aware of for each opportunity.

Since the Fall of Saigon in 1975 until the present day, Vietnam has completely recovered and is producing at near record GDP, while the newly-elected government is gradually issuing a number of initial public offerings of Vietnamese companies. The prospects for our final frontier market to outdo the ASEAN neighbors is what invites the following investment opportunity. The biggest challenge tandem investment and disinvestment in fine Vietnamese equities is actually getting the money into the market. Vietnam's fledgling stock exchange regime has yet to facilitate easy global access - something leading investment indexes are requiring before including Vietnam in their pantheons of international investment opportunities.

CHAPTER 12

Real Estate as a Long-Term Investment

Yes, real estate can be a long-term investment. In the world of real estate investing, like royalty, you have blue bloods and red - third world and emerging market. In emergency land ownership, a new foreigner usually wants a place they call their own. For long-term value, buying and then selling off individual properties are more likely to lose $1,000. However, in the last 15 years, I've never lost a penny in diversified investment portfolios.

Rental properties have easier entry strategies than flipping, despite their complicated reputation. Their costs grow slowly year after year. They need a debt to equity comparison. This means less leverage, but they are diversified as a whole. All would be too risky if you only had three buildings. You either make them a felony or a misdemeanor. REIT can buy like one building at a time. Of all the property classes, only housing has a business format unique to institutional investment.

Many investors dive at West Bank seeking big bucks. While lending practices are typically slower, the safe, get-rich-slow approach has some appeal in the right environment. Loan paydown, rent hikes, and asset appreciation all take place during the process. These objects can be owned more quickly than several homes. There is no objection to someone who desires this path, because the worst-case scenario is that your property gets owned one by one. You're using the same continuing wealth concept. It's not like a boxer's life in a home foreclosure fight, but by thinking like an estate investment class, you can go to bed more peacefully.

Rental Properties vs. REITs

When it comes to long-term investments, rental properties remain the gold standard. At the 2018 Berkshire Hathaway Annual Shareholder Meeting, Warren Buffett called REITs "financial assets." He said, "We like to buy real estate. If we could buy a couple thousand single-family homes, I would love to do that." One of his staff later asked if that was a joke. Warren replied, "No, we are in the business of holding real estate. Not the business of buying a pension fund or a REIT."

Real Estate Investment Trusts are a Vox Investment Group favorite investment, offered through the ETF VNQ, but they offer no compounding factor with dividends. Buy and hold a stock over time, and the seller's basis remains smaller. They do not provide a shelter by deducting dividends until the time of sale. Lots of cash with a high dividend. Eventually, you can invest the dividends in other REITs or stocks. Still, what I have learned managing properties won't change due to taxes or future investments. People will always need real places to live. I can control the Airbnb and work on larger commercial properties at the same time. I currently invest in REITs for passivity reasons. But if I want to make my returns higher, I keep it around 50/50. Any more would reduce the larger real estate portfolio as I couldn't trade larger deals every few days, weeks, or months like I can with my VPN stock. Gear and Kotar are my age? They have just started doing something similar with hotels, I believe.

CHAPTER 13

Retirement Planning and Long-Term Investing

In my book, "How to Endure", I included 4 chapters on retirement and long-term investing, explaining in a bit more detail how to use real assets and business profits to generate enough money at retirement to live the life you want. We considered a range of asset classes: US and international stocks, investment grade municipal and taxable bonds, real estate, and commodities such as gold. On the basis of these assets, we developed four portfolios for retired couples, with 60 years expected life. For the portfolios, we applied an annual inflation rate of 3%.

Portfolio 1 started at retirement, with the couple holding 40% in stocks and 60% in low interest, high-quality bonds. We calculated the total dollar value of the bonds each year, adding that year's inflation rate to inflate the value. The couple invested the stock holdings of their portfolio into stocks of companies. Each year, we added the income from these investments to the bond fund proceeds, and then subtracted the couple's annual budgeted income from the resulting sum. At death, this couple had a positive, absolute increase in portfolio wealth of 20 times their starting portfolio value. That's a $100,000 portfolio achieving a financial value of over $2 million.

And, the couple has been able to withdraw over $100,000 (adjusted for annual inflation) each year for their 60-year retirement! This annual withdrawal rate (AWR) would be expected to exhaust their $100,000 original portfolio in less than 5 years! But, 77 years of compounding growth in their investments gave them the enduring wealth they required. How is that possible?

Strategies for Retirement Income

Non-proprietary wirehouses are harvesting their largest advisors' clients, insurance organizations are pushing annuities into the cash flows of retirees, and private equity firms are selling internal rate of return. The investment industry is all about retirement income these days. Investment professionals go to conferences and read reports from pension consultants at Morningstar and more, or they buy models from fintech companies to budget for an individual or couple spending 4% of their savings each year, increasing the dollar amount with CPI inflation.

In this publication, V.I.C.P.A. discusses popular strategies to generate retirement income in the context of how I think about investing for retirement. We discuss my two-phase model and the mathematics of the Half-Life of Wealth. We will introduce how we leverage our Stock-to-Bond Rotation system to help retirees fine-tune their portfolios and avoid investing retirement benefits in over-valued equity markets if such occasions arise. For the math-inclined reader, we discuss Bond Averaging math and introduce a metaphor.

We are in the midst of an industry-wide shift in the way we, as professionals, discuss the role of a retirement income-generating portfolio in a comprehensive financial plan. And there is no right or wrong way to do it—to create a plan that is unique to each household's spending needs, tax scenarios, and risk tolerances. Because Singletary Financial is exclusively a fee-only investment advisory firm, where we only earn from our clients the single flat annual fee we negotiate and collect in arrears, it is actually easier for us to talk freely about investing our clients' benefits for their phase of the life cycle where money replaces work.

CHAPTER 14

Legacy Planning and Generational Wealth

Effective estate planning is crucial to preserving legacies and maintaining family equilibrium. While tax strategies and the use of family trusts form part of every estate planner's toolbox, high-net-worth individuals also recognize the value of retaining a financial adviser with a roadmap that outlines future investments and planning strategies to ensure their children's future financial needs are secured. It's not just the tax treatment of superannuation from an estate-planning context that is paramount for all. The sustained tax-free growth and notional superannuation details of the death benefit also greatly affect the financial strategies put in place for the children.

The younger the children are, the more benefits they see from further growth following the contribution of a death benefit into superannuation. Consequently, by investing more aggressively within superannuation, parents can take advantage of the further notional gains generated, which could result in tens of thousands of dollars over the child's lifetime. General advice would be to invest in superannuation for a child's lifetime, allowing the notional growth to increase. However, it is also necessary to consider estate-planning strategies before deciding the most relevant financial choice as every situation is different.

As well as managing estates and legacy planning, emotional intelligence – a critical tool when working with clients – is covered as one of the UK's leading advisers, Jane Austen, shares her secret tricks for advisers who lack experience, being mindful of planning strategies for future generations, and being flexible and adaptable in delivering ongoing advice to the next generation. There are several issues that should be considered when succession and legacy planning forms part of a client's financial strategy. These include discussing testamentary trusts and their use as part of inter-generational wealth creation and protection, discretionary and non-discretionary trusts, and whether the client values trusts as a means of providing a smoother and more secure financial future for their dependents. In particular, it is important to consider how notional growth benefits obligations paid from a trust established by a spouse or grandparent are treated for Centrelink purposes, as trust proceeds could affect ongoing and future government entitlements.

Estate Planning Considerations

Estate plans are critical to preserving and passing a lifetime of wealth from one generation to the next. This section will examine some of the tax and other non-tax considerations of importance to wealthy families that make the inter-generational transfer of investments to the next generation of particular interest. Non-tax factors such as the appreciation of extraordinary investments and the fragility of familial relations can be of lesser significance but certainly should not be forgotten in the shuffle for a foothold in the lives and decisions of high net worth individuals. What are the key non-tax factors that the inter-generational transfer of investments can help an investor side-step?

• Systemic risk: inter-generational wealth can provide a hedge against systemic economic forces that reduce the wealth of lower-net-worth families. A broader investment base means that specific investments that lose their value can be offset by similar investments that perform well over the long term, indeed, the very long term! • Divorce: The delegation and potential passing of an investment account will place one household asset beyond the reach of a "spouse-in-waiting or ex-spouse-in-waiting" should a divorce occur. If one can see a dark cloud on a crowded beach, avoiding it can be a prudent hedge. • Contestability, liability protection: An unequally valuable investment account lowers contestability and litigation concerning its potential action • Credit risk: Having large future assets that are divisible between more than one family member acts as a credit hedge for the individual donor, reducing comparative debt level and increasing credit scores, sometimes materially. • Expats: Transferring stock to those who are embarking on international operations can deal with taxation issues triggered by the departure. • Age: Selling to one's children might reduce baby boomers' stock exposure as they start to draw on their RRSPs. What potential disadvantage of transferring exceptional investments from one generation to the next is particularly relevant in this case? An ample estate exempts a deceased taxpayer from an estate obligation, no small consideration. More importantly, though, investment holding company earnings in the next generation would be thereby sheltered, meaning the next generation would have a free hand to directly reinvest their earnings. Such an approach might serve to simplify and systematize the use of investments in a broader investment portfolio. System income, as opposed to a portion of possessing one's system, might lead to family meetings over which investments to profit from the oil and gas sectors versus tech stocks, etc. In a similar vein, if the investments do not perform as predicted, new control mechanisms are available, such as a decrease in plasma or participation in remarkable asset safe-guarded investments federally.

A major role of estate planning generally is to relieve the current owners of their future tax and liability obligations by achieving a tax preferred portfolio structure. This generally involves creating more equity-based investments. Should a single, extraordinary investment account exist which one wishes to avoid owning (and that has no holding company worth creating to cover it), some degree of the inter-generational transfer of investments is still available through the sale of the investment. Keeping in mind that the interest off or renewing some investment portfolios might be given a twenty-year term, a unique investment situation might exist in which selling the investments to one's children would earn a high price. In essence, appreciation that takes a portfolio component out of the owner's estate has now booked. Note that private companies may have more complications as various reserves must be undone on a sale. So while arithmetic may ultimately determine the mechanics, there might be non-arithmetic persuasive reasons on specific investments and to pursue an inter-generational transfer.

CHAPTER 15

Case Studies in Successful Long-Term Investing

I was impressed by an article in June 2017 summarizing the "world's 100 best-performing LPs" over three-year, five-year, 10-year, and 15-year periods. This reinforces the conclusion from the recent academic papers cited above: much of what happens to a long-term investment portfolio is due to events that occurred after it was put together, not before. This is an important truth for those responsible for crafting a portfolio and implementing its investment strategy, and for those cutting them checks.

Case studies rather than theories can offer lessons in investing. In all cases, it should not be concluded that because someone provided these insights, one could easily replicate his results. Rather, the hope is to provide "good advice" as described above. Baron Rothschild said, "The time to buy is when there's blood in the streets." Sir John Templeton provided a compelling case of buying into despair, investing globally and across asset classes, including the undervalued Japanese stock market in the 1960s. Mohnish Pabrai is a devotee of Warren Buffet, claimed to have read much of what Buffet read and attempting to, by careful analysis, quantify good management. He looked everywhere for undervaluation, starting with shabby companies with poor management. Buffet also had the option to do arbitrage, a choice before buying into despair because he had long-term money. Macro Castro bought Brazilian equities about a decade ago after Brazil dropped. After studying Brazil as an economy and a society, he looks for earnings growth rather than low P/E. Smith & Wesson might have been a good time to buy immediately after the college shootings in August, say, some relevant holders of a successful company. That remains to be seen.

Lessons from Prominent Investors

The central objective of this book is to share the essence of prominent investors' experiences in the journey of investing. Insights from their lives can be a good guide for investors. Koch, an extraordinary investor and philosopher, often emphasized hands-on, actual experience. We learn about life through doing things. Time and again, he reiterated this in lectures and talks given on investment management. Investors spend vast sums of money to acquire actual experience, which they think is the key to success. Prominent investors combine theory and actual experience when they address various forums and impart things that matter. Their insights emanate from their experiences. We have learnt a lot from our investment journey. There are four prominent investors with whom I have close association and possibly learnt the most from. These were veterans in their 80s and 90s when I had the pleasure of interacting and discussing the nuances of investing with them.

There are three important parameters we will discuss in the narrative: uncertainty, risk and confidence. All these have a bearing on the process of investment. Each of them, in a way, constitutes a chapter in this edifice. Give an investor 20% of uncertainty arising over a 100 variables, and he will walk away; such a high degree of uncertainty is not acceptable even though unpredictability is prudently accommodated in an investment decision. We would deal with risk in investing. It is not what is attained but what is left over after subtracting what should have been attained from what was actually attained. When people entrusted their wealth with me, I was, in a way, also a man of faith, as investment cannot be in a void. Confidence, therefore, is the cornerstone of investing.

CHAPTER 16

Conclusion: The Journey Ahead

Over the following decades, I carefully laid out the underlying principles and applications of what I call 'value investing' in numerous academic articles, books, and letters. At precisely the moment I began my journey - born amidst a sea of fear that the Great Depression would never end - the financial world began to reap the rewards of a near-endless economic boom, which would continue with few hiccups or interruptions for most of my life. Yet no matter how much the markets have changed over this period, the underlying principles of long-term investing have not. As you have seen, detailed, updated editions of this book abound in best-seller lists and have been translated into dozens of languages. Those volumes contain a great deal of concrete advice and instruction that I hope will continue to guide readers in the future.

My own future likely can't be a mirror image of the path I have taken to get here. For this fifteenth and final section of Enduring Wealth, I offer a sort of conclusion, or past-to-present evaluation, of my journey in long-term investing, which at its heart has been a journey in value investing. I will briefly discuss, in the realm of enduring wealth, the potential paths into the future and possible developments at the crossroads, and will say a final few words to you, fellow long-term investors. The challenge of creating 'enduring wealth' is not a static event; like the markets and the economy, and indeed the world, the book's specifics are evolving. Each chapter comprises a self-contained journey, but I have just suggested they can be read in a fresh sequence to reflect new applications and enduring principles in today's sometimes uncertain realm.

www.ingramcontent.com/pod-product-compliance
Lightning Source LLC
Chambersburg PA
CBHW021355160726
47994CB00007B/2957